She Lives Here
Kristina Hamlett

Unzipped —— Issue 2

She Lives Here
Kristina Hamlett

First published in 2021 by
Life in 10 Minutes Press
Richmond, VA

lifein10minutes.com/press

Distributed by IngramSpark
& Life in 10 Minutes Press

ISBN 978-1-949246-0870

Printed in the United States of America

First Printing, 2021

About *Life in 10 Minutes*

Life in 10 Minutes is a community of writers sharing stories that are brave and true through classes, workshops, retreats, zoom, and our online lit mag. Visit **lifein10minutes.com** to read deep, strange, hilarious, heartbreaking, and powerful stories written 10 minutes at a time, and share yours, too!

Homegrown in Richmond, Virginia, *Life in 10 Minutes Press* began with the mission to give passage to books we believe in. We seek to bring readers titles that are brave, beautiful, raw, heartfelt, and vital, and to nurture authors in their publishing journeys. Learn more at **lifein10minutes.com/press**.

Our mission: We are especially passionate about memoir by women and under-represented voices, nonfiction that challenges the status quo, and boundary-breaking books of all genres. All works published with Life in 10 Minutes Press *are carefully chosen to support our mission and reflect our commitment to promoting fresh, engaging, high-quality storytelling.*

Welcome to *Unzipped*

We are thrilled to introduce *Unzipped* Issue 2, *She Lives Here,* by Kristina Hamlett.

Dive into the lyrical exploration of an innocent girl moving from her close-knit Haitian family in New York to the foreign landscape of the South where she moves from childhood to womanhood, from anger to joy. You'll find fairytales, religious journeys, buffalos and helicopters, butterflies and lions, good grandmothers and bad boyfriends, chocolate and champagne nights.

Coming of age of a writer, and a woman, Kristina navigates the dangerous and toxic messages of a racist and sexist society that dictate who she should be and how she should appear within it. A world where the various messages of religion can either destroy or save you, where she's treated like a Walking Color, from rules enforced by others to the rules she at last chooses for herself. She finds hope and happiness in her body, in other women dancing, in the love of her life, and in celebrating her Whole Black Self.

Join Kristina as she discovers the joy of coming to love herself and the world, along with her family, friends, ancestors, and a God of her own.

Kristina's writing is so luscious and juicy, the joy spills off the page.

Enjoy!
Cindy Cunningham and Valley Haggard, Co–Editors

Contents

I How You Sent Me

continued

2   Whole Black Self

3   She Lives Here

About Alexandra Antoine

Alexandra Antoine is an interdisciplinary artist based in Chicago, Illinois. Her work examines traditional artistic practices throughout the African Diaspora with a focus on healing traditions, identity and culture through the use of collage, portraiture, and most recently, farming. She uses the portrait as a tool to re/present individuals of the African diaspora while exploring her relationship to them within the larger narrative of her Haitian identity. She holds a Bachelor in Fine Arts and Arts Education from the School of the Art Institute of Chicago. Her work has been exhibited throughout the U.S. and is part of the Arts in Embassies program in the U.S. Embassy in Port-au-Prince, Haiti. Visit her at **alexandraantoine.com**.

About the cover art:
While reading Kristina's poetry I am taken on a visual journey of the ways in which love, rage and freedom exist within the Black experience. I'm reminded of the power of nature to heal, the necessities of Black love, laughter and community as well as the evolution of womanhood. Using these themes as a reference I created the collage and painting with vibrant colors in mind to

reflect her Haitian ancestry, architectural elements to represent the spaces and places that have shaped her life, plants to honor the wisdom of nature and linear elements of the Ghanaian adinkra symbol Kojo Baiden recognizing the vision that Kristina has in her understanding of what is to come in her life. It was truly an honor to create these works for such an amazing writer and to be featured within her book.

About Kristina Hamlett

Kristina Cotis Hamlett is a writer, blogger, storyteller and Strongman competitor. She is a graduate of Shenandoah University with a degree in Psychology. She is the author of the E-book journal "What I Love About You: A Guided Journal to Writing Your Proposal and Vows." Kristina's work has been featured on sites such as *kimberlyelise.com, 30seconds.com, Life in 10 Minutes* and *Liminalities*. She currently works in human services and facilitates writing classes at a non-profit organization. She can be found at kristinahamlett.com.

Acknowledgements

Thanks to my husband, Jeff Hamlett, who lets me burst in on him while sleeping and listens to anything I need to share—a fear, a passage, a hope, a poem. His support is unwavering, and his patience is unmatched. Thank you for being my love and my home.

To my parents, Jean and Gina Cotis. You not only gave me life but pushed me to live it—the most loving and compassionate act of parenting.

To my brother, Phillip—my first best friend. Thank you for taking the time to listen and reflect on our memories with honesty and kindness.

To my sister, Jennifer. Thank you for inspiring me to embrace every aspect of my womanhood and look inward first. I cannot thank you enough for always believing in me as a writer (and for buying that laptop for me many years ago). Our sisterhood is one of the things I treasure most in this life.

To my nieces and nephews (Anthony, Adrienne, Cameron, Alana and Marcel)—I do this in part for you. I want you to know that more is possible. It is always the right time to trust yourself and use your voice.

To my extended family—I would not have this well to draw from if it were not for you. The years pass but the memories, they never quite fade. I save a dance for every one of you.

For my grandparents—Yvelle Saintjoy, Etzer and Jacqueline Cotis. It is an honor to be your granddaughter. To my grandmothers, you showed me there is more than one way for Black women to love, sacrifice and show up in this world. Papa Ze, if not for your dedication to record everything, my memories would not be as strong. Thank you for being a keeper of time, a preserver of memories.

Thanks to all my teachers who encouraged my love for reading and writing. To my writing teachers and coach: Valley Haggard, Sadeqa Johnson and Javacia Harris Bowser. To Dr. Boylorn: Thank you for offering your kind words in support of my writing and for amplifying my voice as part of The Storyteller Project.

A special shout out to my friends I have written with: Hope (you saw the poet in me even when I didn't see her in myself), Sheila (a rock whom I depend on for laughter and warmth), Sonia, Kisha, Mary Jo, Arcadia and Veronica.

Thank you to all my friends over the years who have loved, supported and accepted me unconditionally. You know who you are from childhood to VCU, to Shenandoah, DSS, Intercept, OAR, and beyond.

I need to thank my clients I have worked with over the years. You allowed me to experience vulnerability and strength in the face of crisis I may never know. Thank you for allowing me to play a small part in supporting you on your journey.

To my SOGA and See Jane Write family who opened a new world that motivated me to step out from the shadows.

To Alexandra Antoine. Thank you for creating the artwork and listening to my vision. You are wildly talented, my dear friend. The future belongs to you.

Thanks to the team at Life in 10 Minutes Press: Valley Haggard, Cindy Cunningham, Nadia Bukach and Llewellyn Hensley. Being part of *Unzipped* has been a dream realized. Cindy, thank you for being an extraordinary editor. Your insight has been a gift to me. Nadia and Llewellyn, thank you for your time, organization, and hard work to bring this book to life and out into the world. Valley, thank you for calling me that day and asking me to write this collection. You recognized my voice as a scared student walking into your class in 2017 and it has forever changed my life.

Introduction

Writing *Unzipped* meant I wrote this collection despite fear, without apology or explanation. This was not always easy for me to grasp. There is a tiny, pint-sized part of me that wants to backspace this away, rewind to the moment Valley called, send her to voicemail, take my sweet time returning her phone call, only to politely decline, pretending I am happy to walk away from her offer.

I love a good time travel tale, but this is not one. I did pick up the phone and what transpired was a confirmation of what I already knew to be true. This year I asked myself to be honest and what came of it broke my heart wide open, embarrassed me, enraged me and often begged me to find the closest pen and paper to no longer hold it inside. My stories are "urgent, brave and true" to me, a woman who catches herself hiding behind words, tucking away the raw, juicy, ugly in the middle hoping you may accidentally skip over it. To stop hiding, I asked myself to tap into my fullness. The confirmation came because just as I was telling myself I could not be alone, that phone call came asking me to share these stories. I have not believed in coincidence for quite some time. But God, bending and breaking of the rules, kindness, our ability to adapt to our benefit and to our destruction and an all-consuming love of Black women who birthed me, challenged me, fed me, broke me and put me back together again—yes, I believe in those things.

Coincidence—no.

Intention—yes.

I wrote this with intention.

1

How You Sent Me

My roots run deep.
I have been nourished well.

—Assata Shakur

How You Sent Me

Flaky Haitian beef patties wrapped in parchment paper,
packed in white boxes from the bakery.

Dirty sidewalks in the Bronx

Watch out for the diaper!

Off to the corner store with our nickels for Jolly Ranchers
and Now and Laters

Rehearsing "Push It" and "Hold On" so we could be our own
girl group

Playing in Melissa and Diana's father's study

May-lisa Mommy Jacotte said, sweetly singing her name.

Riding the bus with my grandmother

Climbing the tree in Nennen Evelyn's backyard on Long Island

Spinning around the beam in their basement

Barbecues for birthdays with cake, rice, beans, chips, chicken,
burgers, corn on the cob

Air thick with spice and smoke

Plastic cups with *Barbancourt* rum and the whisper of ice

Made-up faces in floral dresses and shorts and braids and sweaty t-shirts

From tag and choreographed dances and my auntie

Gave us the grandest of introductions.

We were stars.

and Scenario, oh Scenario, do you know the words?

How fast can you rap it?

Are you Q-Tip mellow or roaring like Busta Rhymes?

My brother and I with Nenenn Guetty as she praised God in her bedroom, and we would sing together:

I love You, more than anything, I love you, more than anything. I praise You, more than anything. Lord, I give my life to you.

Ascending the steps to my cousin Marc's bedroom to see his
Bob Marley poster.

I looked for it every time.

Holding onto the edge of a windowsill in our apartment as I walked on my knuckles, taking pride in the dexterity of my toes.

I thought this was ballet.

We were in Springfield,

Crossing the street between my cousins' homes.

Hugging a Cabbage Patch doll with orange yarn hair on the first day of school, my name tag pinned to my blouse before entering PS 101.

Shopping on Jamaica Ave

Parties at Jean-Robert's club

We were all lace and ribbons, full skirts, jumping and swinging
our little hips.

Tabou Combo horns and rhythms blaring from the speakers

A mix of Kompa, salsa and merengue with the occasional American
feature directing our feet

Thick black pigtails and barrettes, bouncing along our shoulders,
grazing our back

We were on a train.

Auntie took us to Lincoln Center and my mouth was open, gaping,

At the grandeur of the tree and because I spied a young couple
kissing beneath it.

Our small bodies thought we owned the night,

On a sparse subway platform

With a lone rat scurrying across

Because we were with New York way past bedtime, breaking dawn.

Watching Gardy walk down the sidewalk from work, waiting for our
dollar for the ice cream truck on the brick steps at the house on 109th

Catching fireflies with Cherry from next door

The black mesh skirt with multi-colored bows my cousin let me keep
as she was cleaning out her closet at the brownstone in Flatbush.

She was glamour.

It took years for me to throw it away.

Learning and then promptly forgetting to swim at a Queens YMCA

Fernando and Loretta coming over, lit cigarettes in the apartment

Hall and Oates on the radio

So much jump rope my feet blister at the memory.

"Down Down Baby" and "Miss Mary Mack", hands clapping furiously, faster and faster

I remember it all.

These shreds, pieces, shards, layers, folds, slivers of images, notes of magic, static and moving

New York

You gave me roots.

You made me

With your imperfect people, your aversion to silence, your accent, your grime, your pace, your heat

You sent me to Virginia

a spoiled little girl.

What Did She See?

My grandmother, Yvelle, running in a mango grove, the skirt of her plaid school uniform whipping around her. She takes off her shoes, stuffs her lace-trimmed socks into them, and shoots off the second she stands up. Her mud brown feet come to an abrupt stop underneath a large tree with lush leaves, brimming with fruit. Its low hanging branches just barely tickle her scalp, and her toes make lazy circles in the earth as she gazes up at the plump treasures dangling within reach. She stretches her small arms and fingers to pull down the succulent, fragrant mango. Once she peels the auburn and red ripe skin, she sinks her teeth into the ginger flesh.

I always picture the innocent start to her life. I picture her without the pain—the inevitable, searing pain that none escape. I yearn to know that part. Her before. The husband and subsequent abuse. The affairs and the children. Meeting and the losing the love of her life, my mother's father. Her sojourn to America with her fragmented English—one word in her new tongue for every three in her old. The grandchildren and illnesses. And certainly, long before her death in a Virginia hospital.

I often wonder if she did the same, if she painted pictures of us—of who and how we were, of

who we would become. Was I the image she pictured of her children in the Haitian Diaspora?

Dec. 6, 1992   7th
Byrd.
Henrico.

I have notebooks and notebooks of pages containing my thoughts and feelings. Right now, I look back at the phrases I used and hope I will capture those graceful thoughts again. My eyes catch my words in a captivating hypnotic gaze in a way that is undescribable. I intend to abduct it from the past and take it on a journey to the future. More meaning that I will continue my past fantasies, making them coherent, and stimulating to any reader. I want to write humorous creative commercials along with stories that deep, mature people can really enjoy.

Excerpt from Kristina Cotis's middle school journal, December 6, 1992.

The Cottage

Anyway, I plan to be a virgin all my life,
wrap myself around literature,
every aspect or phase of it.

—Kristina Cotis, 11 years old.

Long before I knew maladaptive daydreaming,

It knew me.

I was caught mouthing words to myself well into my 20s.

I was always dreaming of another way,

the other Kristina would do it.

She would wear this V-neck blouse and these skin-tight jeans,

Her smile would gleam brighter, her nails impeccable, lips glossy,

Hair shiny, bouncy, full

Witty with eyes cutting to the left or the right on time

Riding a beat perfectly or pressed against someone

A performance.

It's more fun in your head.

My brain says.

I always knew I

Was this way.

Even as an 11-year-old

On black roller skates with yellow wheels

Skidding across the kitchen floor

Down the plastic runner in the foyer

Always someplace else

Drifting off to my future

All grown up

Living in a cottage in Vermont

Nestled in the forest

Sipping cocoa on winter mornings

In the springtime

Perched near a window

Drinking in

Morning inspiration

Eating nothing but a bowl of grapes

Anyone could tell

I was an intense writer, a single, virginal woman hunched over her desk.

No time for men. Only for words

With a furrowed brow,

Scribbling furiously into notebooks

Sometimes a quill pen with an ink well would appear on my desk and a

Cream, wool blanket draped over my shoulders.

My book was about a writer named Alena who was the best novelist at the "company" (not at the publishing house), and they were terrified to lose her.

Alena lunched with friends at the café where the talk of the day was love, sex, and politics. They teased my independent woman for being a woman with no man.

They just didn't get it.

Alena was an independent woman.

I was an independent woman.

They would see, when I arrive at school to make speeches and people would chant my name.

They'd understand.

What it takes

To be a serious writer!

I forgot all about this little girl until I was 31, sitting at my wedding reception. My brother gave a toast where everyone, including me, roared with laughter at the tale of an 11-year-old Kristina who claimed she would never be married or have sex but wrap herself up in literature and eat grapes in her cottage and is now seated next to her husband—no cottage or Vermont or grapes in sight— but a writer's heart still beating beneath the white dress.

Standing on Ceremony

1. *Catholic*

I was eight the first time I walked into mass,
Across from the ocean.
Committing "Our Father" to memory
There would be a First Communion
and a Father Mike to confess
Our deep, dark secrets to
in hopes of
Forgiveness

First Communion Day
Off to the salon
Bangs framing my tiny brown face
Thick freshly shaped brows

Head crowned and hair sprayed curls peeking through

A veil flowing down my mane

Nennens and uncles drove down from New York

Cakes in the shapes of lamb and princess for all

Lacy, glittery dresses with full skirts to twirl in

Feet adorned with stockings burn up the beige carpet

Sweating out bangs and braids

My grandfather memorializes our every movement on his camcorder.

Mommy Jacotte snaps and claps,

Grabs us by the hand, swings our arms.

She is caught in his frame.

It burns brightest

This night

Ceremony has faded away.

My only confession:

A late homework assignment

My penance forgotten.

I tell myself now Father Mike laughed to himself

After I exited the

Confessional

***

2. Pentecostal

Here we shout

Bodies lose consciousness

Wriggle and convulse on carpet

No priest to place

A Communion wafer on my tongue and

Press a wine cup to my lips.

Here people know the future

Prophet and Prophetess

A woman we know dreams of a husband

Buys a wedding dress that collects dust in her closet.

Here we speak in tongues.

We catch the Holy Spirit.

No crossing the chest with my right hand

On my left side

Holy Ghost

Makes a grand entrance

And I

Will utter celestial languages

Meant only for God

And those with the gift

Of Interpretation.

Baptism

No sprinkles allowed.

Full immersion

My hair will be wet and for the first time

not because of the pool or wash day

We are in robes.

Mommy is proud.

I was reborn.

Where are you, Holy Ghost?

Where is your fire?

I don't want to go to hell.

Hands laid on me at children's church.

Prayer meetings

Holy Ghost Fire on everyone but

Me

Over shouts, stomping of feet.

Let me catch the wave.

My brother caught it.

I never did.

***

3. *"The One True Church"*

Where it all went quiet
We sing, unaccompanied and off-key.
No instruments
Woman
No, you cannot be a pastor.
No, you cannot be an elder.
No, you cannot be a deacon.
You cannot teach a man.

My baptism—worthless
I had to be reborn
Again
Context disappears.
We are New Testament
The world outside of our doors
Is on their own.
You know where everyone else is going.
Straight to hell.

My mother acts like she doesn't hear that part.
We are of and with our family and friends still.
My mother loves Sunday morning, Sunday night,
Wednesday night for us.
Now we have structure.

Isn't that what we always wanted?

Where is joy?
I cannot find it.
I cannot detect it.
I keep having to push
Shame, boredom and self-righteousness aside
It keeps blocking my view of the joy
That must be there.

No tongues,
You poor, deceived soul.
Tongues, Holy Ghost Fire
Has been extinguished.
You were in a fantasy.
None of it was real.

Dancing
Swaying
even with my father and grandfather
May be leading an innocent onlooker
Down a wicked path
Tempting them with my movements
Abandon
Your
Culture

***

4. *Goodbye*

Hiding from the world

Hurts

By pretending we are not

Of the world

As if we don't commune with, laugh with, whisper our deepest
and our darkest to

Seek adventure with

Aunts, uncles, friends, boyfriends, cousins, teammates, girlfriends,
neighbors, co-workers

As if we cocooned ourselves

In a universe

With holy, impenetrable shields

Never appears to match

Reality

Those shields were

Gossamer—flimsy, see-through.

We feared the world.

Hands and feet of God

Without extending

Those hands and feet

Is a

Lie

Goodbye

To people

Who wouldn't give freely

Of themselves

Unless

The strangers in need

Believed as they do.

Striving for stainlessness

Is a hardship.

Little acceptance

But a bounty of secrets

Grace was a mystery to me.

Our lives

Intertwined

We broke bread,

Went to movies, prayed for our sick, our grieving, sent care packages.

I still want to protect those people.

A tenderness still exists.

But we kept standing on ceremony.

***

5. *Now*

Walking through new doors

Nothing like the old

Yearning

For brothers and sisters in pews

For community

I'd give it time

And then

Something always falls apart

Namely trust.

I ask myself

Am I waiting for a group of fallible humans to become infallible?

Assigning myself judge, jury and executioner.

Am I asking them to achieve a state of perfection I never will?

I don't know where God is in that ask.

An Offering

She is mother's mother.

Matriarch and Patriarch

She is ancestor.

She is mortar and pestle on the kitchen counter.

Mayi moulen simmering on the stove

Floral and paisley printed on her skirts

Chanel lingering on her skin

Morning stretches in a pink muumuu

Gazing at the miracle of Mother Mary on the wall,
clutching her rosary.

She is a survivor who crossed oceans so the world could see

Her.

Throwing her head back while laughter and music floated
from her throat

Joy unearthly

And we are tiny hands massaging her feet during Dallas
and Falcon Crest on Friday nights

And we are sitting between her legs as she greased,
parted and braided many a crown.

She is slicing with deft hands, avocado as an offering to us.

the shape of her mouth as she said *Ah-vo-ca-do*.

Haiti never left her.

Her presence made brothers and sisters out of cousins.

Her essence made brothers and sisters out of cousins.

She rests.

And I offer

These words to her.

Lines Drawn

We draw lines

Down the middle.

You go here.

You belong there.

Even when we don't like it.

My earliest lines drawn

Between two women

My grandmothers

Veve and Mommy Jacotte

Yvelle and Jacqueline

Born in Haiti

Immigrated to New York

Flew without their loves

With children alongside of them

For different reasons.

Many summers with them
Brother, sister, me.

Lines drew themselves.

Father's mother
Dutiful wife
Floral muumuus with netting covering rollers.
Cooking breakfast
Buttery vermicelli pasta with onions and bananas
Filled my plates.

Time to be dressed.
Ammens powder dusted on our bodies.
Braiding hair and tying ribbons over barrettes
Colorful spools, silver scissors
Housed in the navy Royal Dansk cookie tin.

We were pretty dolls.
Rambunctious dolls
She was made up.
Dresses fit over ample frame.
A long single strand necklace with a miniature gold globe

And a gold band
Adorning neck and fingers

Her Queens backyard
A train hovering over us
Endless parties
With rice cooked
Harmony of music, laughter
She was twirled by my grandfather
When he did not have a camcorder
hoisted over a shoulder.

Image, perception
Beauty, reputation
Always meant
Everything
Unmarried women living with men
Were called "wives."
Watchful eyes
Kept over my appearance.
Fraught with worry
If my ears were bare

***

Who I Know Now

Frail
Quieter
Hair coiffed underneath wigs
And perfectly powdered face
Fret over her
Take care of her.

I beg my memory
Not to fail me
Not to fail her
She was more
Than
Cartoonish Caribbean Stepford wife
Stirring rice and beans
Tranpe and marinating meat
Making us all pretty

She hustled
between buses and cabs
So, we could be with people
Who were of her, too.
She lost so much
Before my father was born

I am ignorant

Of what it is

To be a working mother alone

For a year

While your love goes ahead of you

To forge a new life

In a new country

You begged us

Speak to me.

I need to learn English.

A driver's license acquired

Without a real use for it.

She gave us children to play with because

She had no other grandchildren for us at her home.

But there was an intermingling

Veve and Mommy Jacotte

Elizabeth Arden for two months

Working together

Birthdays, holidays

Religious traditions

Honored together.

***

VeVe

Mother's mother

She was teacher.

She was mother.

Nine babies, two of which never got to grow.

She was glue

Holding chaotic familial energy

Together

Many households within

One house

She welcomed us onto her lap

Before the ravaging of strokes and diabetes

I cannot morph her

Into a Stepford wife.

This avenue

Was never available to her.

She was

Work together

Live together

Figure out this life

Together.

No façade

To keep up

No charades

Europe, Central America, South America

Saw her.

Many times

She hopped trains

To see

Her superstar,

Andre the Giant

And wrestlers grapple and tragically overact

At Madison Square Garden.

Her vibrancy lingers.

I do not speak to the dead

Revive spirits

The other has gone quiet.

Mystery remains.

I have tried

Drawing out syllables

Raising and lowering of

Decibels

I am not understood.

She says

I love you.

I miss you.

Happy you called.

Comes alive

To speak of her pain

Expresses glee

at financial gifts

Offers kissing sounds

As goodbyes

***

Where It Leaves Me

Expectations swept away.

Limitations accepted.

I am Auntie now.

In 30 years

my hope is to be called,

to be received with patience

as I recount stories

Inspire them

With travels

Dreams chased

Warn them of those

Deferred

Slip in my woes about elderly aches

I loved them both.

I love them both.

These women who led

Disparate lives.

But collided.

For the love of children.

It erases lines drawn.

Balance

Ages 9-12

2 shakes and a sensible

Dinner

Fasting for "spiritual" purposes.

Praying to subtract more of myself.

Craving a lean, flat stomach

And telling my future pastor's wife I want to be thin enough

to wear a bikini (that I never wore)

I can still see her expression after I said it.

Tight with worry and judgment.

Admonished loudly by my father for wanting a slice of leftover pizza
hours before Thanksgiving dinner.

I meant shamed.

my older cousin's wife

joking about how fat I was while standing with a group of my other cousins because we were teasing my brother for being too skinny.

We were wrong and *We* were teasing.

I was the fat one.

my uncle's wife

watching me run after my little cousin, her daughter, at a Christmas Expo, trying to corral her, get her to be a good girl who stands still.

She said to me:

"Good, maybe you'll lose some weight."

After 12

A white neighborhood in a new city

Weight Watchers

Cabbage Soup Diet

The Grapefruit Diet

Fasting again

2 workout videos at night

Weight Loss Forever (the one that made me stop inhaling sausage and cheese biscuits and Diet Dr. Pepper for breakfast at school)

Age 15—Buying hot dogs, a snack pack of Fig Newtons and peach sweet iced tea at the 7-11 in the shopping center of my afterschool job before coming home to eat dinner because I had money now and no one could tell me I couldn't eat.

Now you can't watch me.

Now you can't stop me.

My father, telling me in a booth with cracked red vinyl seats in a dimly lit Chinese restaurant that I had a pretty face, but no one would want me because I was too big.

Maybe a big, tall Black man one day.

I was 16.

He was only trying to help.

My father telling me, after one of my running phases, that I was finally starting to look "normal."

He was only trying to help.

The one with the fat burning cookies and the blond woman in her 50's who used to measure my body in her office, a small guest house in the backyard, her large prowling dog who barked and growled at me during every visit.

Holistic diets that work until I want bread and decide to forget how "broccoli is a broom that sweeps away the toxins from my intestines."

Pretending that eating the whole cake except the chocolate frosting lining the perimeter of the box is doing good.

Bannann peze, chicken thighs, rice, beans and a cold, frosty bottle of Cola Champagne

While watching "The Biggest Loser"

Watching all the weight loss porn that ever existed and convincing myself I am not pairing a hearty side of judgment with my viewing.

Am I bigger than them? I am now smaller than them. How can they let themselves get so big? I feel sorry for them.

Hiding night eating. Not talking about night eating.

Not eating lunch

Drinking coffee for lunch

Drinking lemonade for dinner after miles of running

Vegetarianism with miles of running, a larger plate of food with a side salad for lunch and large plate of salad with a salad bowl of food for dinner at the cafeteria in college

Whole 30

Terrified of the scale so my sister weighs me and writes down the number to pass to me

Because I can't bear to hear the number out loud.

How I could have made her a part of that?

Weighing myself in the day and in the night

down 29 up 42 down 73 up 26 down 34 and up and up and up

Ignoring the scale

Veganism, alkaline vegan, raw vegan, junk food vegan—what I do now because the bones after I devoured a chicken years ago morphed into a carcass before my eyes as I threw them away.

No alcohol, a gallon of water, thousands of dollars with a doctor to learn about sugar and carb counting and supervised workouts and weigh-ins.

Working out three times in a day

Once until my thighs locked up, frozen and I was fearful

I wouldn't be able to rise from the couch.

What is balance?

A Time Gone By

There was a pocket of time in my life where I spoke up in class.

I made friends with people from all over the planet.

I ran miles every day. I felt almost guilty for eating, for even speaking to others until I got my run in.

I wore glasses.

I straightened my hair, continuing in the tradition of what I was trained to do with my own head.

I flirted too much. I was friends with a group of guys who used to call me Ms. Mocha.

I went to musicals and opera recitals. I danced every week. I did handstands in yoga class.

I fell in love with someone who never loved me back, someone who could make my throat dry up and stomach flutter simultaneously.

I traveled to Costa Rica.

When I or a friend was heartbroken, we threw Chocolate and Champagne nights.

I said goodnight in Japanese to my roommate.

I spoke about August Wilson.

I had two close friends but had a sneaking suspicion
I was the third wheel.

I sauntered for no reason.

2

Whole Black Self

I can see a sunny place—
Life exploding green
i can see your bright, bronze skin
at ease with all the flowers
and the centipedes.

—Assata Shakur

Sometimes hope
is the biggest weapon of all
to use against us.

—Edwidge Danticat

A Party

I dreamt of

Toiling and frolicking in the sun

Together

I dreamt of us

Around the table

Eating the fruits of our labor.

Leafy greens massaged with marinade

Inviting mangoes sliced

And plantains sweet

To the party.

I dreamt of

Brown faces,

Smiling with mouths open.

Diving

"We never forgot about you."

"We came looking for you."

"And we found you."

I heard those words in a video around 1:30am. I had one blank page left in a brown leather-bound journal on my side table. I wrote those words down because I never want to forget them.

It was spoken by a diver. She is a member of a group: Diving with a Purpose. Their mission is to deep dive into oceans on the hunt for shipwrecked vessels that once held captive Africans. They teach people how to measure the ship, collect vital information and preserve history. These men and women, many of whom are Black, felt compelled to learn to dive, become guardians of history to find us.

Those who never made it.

Those who chose the sea.

I wept a little as I watched.

Their resolve was clear.

Their bravery and curiosity stoked flames in me.

What will I dive deep for?

What will I fight to preserve?

What will I not let slide anymore, desperate to believe he or she or they "didn't really mean it?"

What is my battle cry?

What will I live for?

What am I willing to die for?

I will live, die, cry, fight

And write

To protect my peace,

My people.

Anything else

Is not worth diving for.

It's Called Anger

When I punch the air

It doesn't land.

I need something to connect

With my fist.

Maybe it would ease the burn

In my chest.

Cool it down.

That's too much, Kristina.

Why are you like this?

I am like this because I am sure I swallowed the white supremacy
that I was force fed.

Our "great" forefathers

The "discovery" of the Americas

I cannot even face all the slop I have had to regurgitate.

Instead of the Black excellence

I've identified as Christian

And today I heard a pastor refer to their privilege

As "White Blessings."

I hope you choke on it

And it goes down like serrated knives.

I am like this because my niece is scared for my life.

My life.

I want to tell her it's not true. Her fear is completely irrational.

But I promised to be a truth teller.

I hate watching children protest,

Clutching and raising their homemade signs.

Not because of their awareness.

But because they are supposed to revel in their innocence.

It was NEVER supposed to be their turn to march
about strange fruit.

I hate that I know there are other Black people

Ancestors not born in Amerikkka

Who don't recognize their Blackness.

You are BLACK.

You are BLACK.

You are Blackity BLACK.

Your first language, your gorgeous accent, your work ethic,
your degrees WILL NOT SAVE YOU.

They are not a shield.

Wake up from your slumber!

Your BLACKNESS burns

So damned bright.

Don't be afraid.

Don't believe what they told you.

AND I SHOUT THIS

As a Haitian American woman.

You can own your BLACKNESS and your culture.

Your kinky hair, your Kompa, Zouk, accent, lips, pwa, jollof

Your hips, your heritage, your melanin, your joy,

The honor of your family name.

They can live in the same place.

They have to.

We were enslaved and colonized

A world apart.

Don't forget it.

We are cousins.

I hate that I know there are some

Whose ancestors were

Enslaved in Amerikkka,

Terrified of change,

Of being accused of being "too Black."

Don't want to rock the white supremacy boat.

And because of your fear, you spout tired and false claims about Black-on-Black crime and won't look your Brothers and Sisters in the eye.

The flames in my chest that roar

The melancholy that invades

Because all who are lost will not be found.

Athlete Ready?

No one tells a fat, 39-year-old Black woman with breaking skin
and aching joints

that it's time to become an athlete.

Didn't you know?

It is time for her to take a seat and consider what to buy next,
which diet to try—they have a list for you.

tell you who or what to hurl your fury at,

which show

or man

or woman

or book is to become your next

obsession.

Nevertheless

At 39, I reached for the knob and turned the noise down
with such ferocity that it

Broke

Anything

To turn down that noise

Because if I could hear that list or you tell me which thing
is to be my next

obsession

I wouldn't have been able to hear

A trainer ask what sports I used to play, which division 1 sport
did I play?

Massage my ego.

Make me pliable

But I heard her

And told her no. never any sports.

I have never competed.

I would have never heard her tell me

I was strong, the muscle buried beneath this fat waiting to lift
and pull and carry astounds her.

I would not have heard her tell me

Now you will be able to jump those boxes.

Turn it down a little more.

Now I can hear

"Athlete Ready?"

I lift 65 pounds 16 times in a minute over my afro,
eyes beseeching the sky for more strength,

Pull rope, hand over hand, seated in a giant tire,

until I can no longer feel the burning in my palms,

dragging a weighted sled across Astroturf to me with all my might

With my back to a net, fling weighted balls over it repeatedly,

Hauling a 100lb husafell 50 ft pinned to my chest w/ rapid tiny steps,

Daring to deadlift 315lbs

With a crowd, half full of strangers,

None of whom are fat 39-year-old Black women.

Now I mute it.

So, I can hear my name

When they announce I've placed 3rd

And now it's OK to turn it all the way up

Because they can scream whatever they want,
add some boom and bass and a solo

I can no longer hear it.

Because I am now in the mirror.

And a beautiful, Black 39-year-old full woman with chalky palms,
bruised forearms, broken nails and a medal hanging from her neck

Is staring back at me.

And we were four...

For T, C, and B

We were four.

Two men and two women.

Surrounded by earth—green, soft and growing.

Feet and feet and feet and feet and feet and feet apart.

To keep each other alive.

The men spoke of their sons

And time needed to miss

10 tiny fingers

10 tiny toes

And toddler voices.

They spoke with a fondness

Only reserved for men who love.

One woman swirled a hula hoop around her hips

And I perched on a red chair, taking us all in.

We had an easy peace

The kind that is only honed over time,

Even after months of being apart.

We were minding our own business

Bidding a farewell to one of our own

We heard it before we saw it.

An intruder

An uninvited guest

Flying above us

Blue "X" thirteen white stars angry red

Pummeling God's great sky

A banner with hate you hope was meant for the shadows

Whipped behind it, assaulting the wind.

A coward's way of asserting

Dominance

Our eyes cast upwards.

One of us stalked the plane from the ground,

Daring it to make a landing.

To square up

face to face

My mind's eye saw us

Ascend into the air

Transformed, wielding katanas, draped in kimonos.

We were all

Yasuke, the 16th century African samurai

Our blades splitting the banner,

Slicing through hot metal

Crashing it to the green

Where our easy peace once lived.

Through billowing smoke and sweat, the bloody pilot

Pleads for our mercy.

"Hear us."

We declare.

"This is not a time for mercy."

And we hung

Suspended

Mid-air

The last of that coward

His banner, flag and plane

Burning

Already a fading memory to us

And we were four.

Two men.

Kristina Hamlett

Two women.

Owning our peace

Bidding a farewell.

Family

One told me my skin, along a continuum of brown was beautiful.
My Black is Beautiful.

Another tells me that *lakay* means home and Aux Cayes possesses
almost forgotten, almost sanded off imprints of my DNA.

Attached myself to people who call themselves Greats and to
another who picked up the Pen and put the Fears down.

So many names I have gone by:

Great, Black, Brown-Skinned, Haitian, American, Haitian American,
Writer, African American, Christian, Woman, Wife, Sister, Natural.

I am a member. I fell in. I joined. I paid. I listened. I spoke up. I have
shouted. I have risen. I have sat down. I have dreamed. I have
cowered. I have fallen. I have kneeled with purpose. I have prayed.
I have cursed. I have written.

I was born.

Within these families, these families, I am human. I have found my
humanity and I find myself extending my hand to touch yours.

We. Are. Supernatural.

preface to A Walking Color

It has been said we all have angels assigned to us or all around us.

If that is true, mine sent me to the University of Tuscaloosa, Alabama in October of 2018.

I was chosen, along with 14 other women across the country to participate in a three-day workshop: The Storyteller Project: Digital Storytelling for Women of Color facilitated by Robyn Boylorn and Veralyn Williams with a special lunch and learn with Dr. Rachel Raimist.

When I was selected, I remember feeling so much excitement I paced the room. I didn't even think about what it would be or who I would be in that space until I got the additional information we needed to prepare before coming — "Bring an excerpt written by/about a woman of color that inspires or resonates with you (one paragraph or less). Personal story ideas or topics (Consider what part of your story do you want to tell and why?)"

That part of the preparation made it real. I was going to come and fellowship, yes. But I was going to have to do the work.

It demanded that one of my truths be spoken.

As time passed and the workshop was rescheduled from August to October, I had time to let a few doubts seep in about whether my story would be compelling or impactful enough, but I never let it take up residence in my mind, the only place that matters.

Within seconds of arriving in The Hub at The University of Alabama, any fears I had were allayed. I was met with such warmth by the other women, Dr. Boylorn and her graduate assistant, Lola, I was instantly at ease. I no longer doubted the validity or the strength of my story. There was no reason to wonder why I had been chosen.

There was no time for my "stuff."

I witnessed Black women being daughters, Black women being mothers and Black women being sisters.

Black women giving ourselves permission to fall apart recognizing someone was there to provide a soft place, lap and heart.

I witnessed women give birth to their stories.

It was painstaking at times, but it was healing.

There were women aching to release their screams, aching for the women who raised them, aching to claim their sexuality, aching for healing, aching to tell stories of other silenced and forgotten Black men and women, aching to be seen and aching for a way to grieve.

There were moments when my heart was so full, "overflow" will never be the word, is not enough of a word.

On Day 1, we were asked to work in groups to talk about Black women, our stories and address the themes of the passages we brought.

By Day 3, it was evident they were not just words in marker on paper taped to a wall. We gave those words life. We breathed life into those words. We embodied those themes and stories in our work.

I was in a room full of survivors.

Veralyn Williams came from New York to start co-facilitating with Robin help us produce our audio/audiovisual stories. In addition to sharing her own expertise, she challenged me. I had never used the iMovie application and was frustrated trying to navigate it. After helping me with some of the more difficult parts of the editing process, she let me know in no uncertain terms she was not going to complete it for me.

Even though I did not ask her to, she knew if I sat back and let her continue to work on the visuals, I would have. It became glaringly obvious how uncomfortable I am with people recognizing my fear of not being able to do something well.

After dinner and pictures, we all sat together to screen our stories and enjoy cake.

I know I can only speak for myself but what I experienced during and especially after the screening was no less than supernatural.

When a group of Black women who don't hold shame and celebrate the skin they are in congregate and create with love, there is a sense of power, a collective power in the room.

We. Are. Supernatural.

Awkward, soft, strong, honorable, brash, intelligent, sexy, artistic, quiet, curious, unapologetically ambitious, feminine, nerdy, funny as hell but supernatural, nonetheless.

Right before coming, I was in the middle of a serious healing journey with my husband. I considered not coming.

I made the right choice.

I chose my voice.

I chose to welcome new ones into my life.

Here is the story I want you to know.

A Walking Color

In 1989, I was in 4th grade. I went to a newly built school with too many children and not enough classrooms. Their solution was to have classroom trailers. Our teacher tried many configurations of class. She split us down the middle, so our desks were facing one another one day and the next we were all facing her.

One day, she decided to ask us to arrange all our desks in a square. I don't remember if it was that specific day but soon afterwards, she announced to the entire class how beautiful she found Black people's smiles to be. She loved how white our teeth are.

She then encouraged the Black children to open our little mouths and smile. All 3 of us. Show the class our teeth. All I can remember was confusion as I reluctantly parted my lips and opened my mouth. My smile wasn't much better or worse than anyone else's. I looked at the other two Black kids, Thomas and Marcus, feeling panic.

But their mouths were open, too.

It felt like we were being inspected for auction, as if at any moment she would put her pale, shriveled fingers on my cheeks and pry my mouth open wider for the crowd to see, to ooh and ah.

She stood there, smiling and waited for all our classmates to get a good look.

After it was over, another child asked me why our smiles were better and what was wrong with hers? I don't remember my answer. I didn't know and that's what I probably told her.

I wondered why she felt the need to do that to us. Especially her. The first day I saw my teacher, I was shocked by her face. It was apparent she had been in a horrific accident and the skin on her cheeks seemed withered. I learned later she had been thrown from a horse years ago. She wore copious amounts of foundation and blush to cover it up, but it was there.

Why would someone who was plagued by something she couldn't hide, something I am sure made her feel vulnerable, put innocent children in that position?

I know what the truth is. She didn't see us at all.

To her, we were walking colors.

You may be wondering what the fallout was from that incident.

There was none. I said nothing. I am betting little Thomas and Marcus stayed quiet, too.

I didn't even think to say anything to my mother and father.

I now realize it was trauma. I froze in the classroom and buried it deep. My 8-year-old body, my 8-year-old brain did what it could. Pushed it down and didn't speak of it. Pushed down the confusion. Pushed down the feeling of wanting to be swallowed up by the Earth. Pushed down not being safe in the care of my teacher.

Of course, a part of me wishes I had at least said no or kept my mouth closed and marched to the principal's office, but 8-year-old Kristina didn't even realize she had the right. She didn't realize she had complete ownership over her body in any space.

I didn't know until then that people didn't see me.

They could choose not to see me.

They couldn't see my Blackness was one piece, one part, one curve, one edge, one angle.

I have a voice now. I can speak up for her. Even when speaking up feels like I am screaming into a void, I can speak up for 8-year-old Kristina now.

I am not a walking color.

I am not a walking color.

I am not a walking color.

I am not a Black robot that walks and talks. I am a Haitian American woman, born in Queens, New York. Hearing two languages spoken around me was my norm. Rice and beans are my norm.

I became a Southerner by moving to Virginia Beach at age five. I never became a Southern belle. That is not me.

I cry when I pray.

I laugh so hard I snort.

I dance by myself.

I played pretend. I built forts with my brother and took pictures on the beach with my sister.

I crushed on boys who didn't like me and avoided some who did.

I have gained and lost hundreds of pounds.

I am married. I am madly in love with my best friend, my husband. I fear for his health sometimes. I joke and tell him we are going out of this world together, hands clasped together on the same bed, Notebook style. I will be 100. You will be 110. Them's the rules! I joke in an awful country accent.

I wear an afro.

Reading was my first love.

I have swallowed more rage than I can recount since I was a little girl because to some people, I am a walking color.

I am a walking color.

I just want to be seen as whole, flawed and love.

I want you to see the God in me.

I see Him in you.

Whole Black Self

My Black self is a whole human being

Who wants to celebrate other Black people

Who wants to binge on Black everything

I crave Black expression.

Who wants to sit on my damn couch eating banana bread

My Whole black husband baked.

My Black self

Took a walk this morning,

Made sure I stared right into the eyes of two Black men walking in our neighborhood and shouted a robust

"Good morning!"

And what I hoped I said was "I see you!"

My Black self cried and checked on friends.

I ignored the deafening silence today from people who should have been screaming along.

And those who proclaimed, "This is how you protest."

My Whole Black spirit wrestles with defeat when I think of Black businesses who may never open again and Black people

Who will never breathe again.

My Whole Black self will pray, make love to my Whole Black husband and fall asleep,

Wake up

In a rage

And do it all over again.

3

She Lives Here

Should is a dangerous word.
—Allan Loeb

It's not in our hearts to hold our destinies to ourselves.
—Eugene Ashe

Time wasn't ready for me and I wasn't ready for time.
—Pharrell Williams

Fireflies

I watched fireflies

Dance

Through blades of grass

Kiss

The bark of a tree

Luminate

The sky

And I was

Jealous

They seemed to

Be more free

Than

Me.

The Rules

Three-quarter length sleeves

Hem at the knee

Bare arms can be shown at the beach

And inside the home only.

Large T-shirts that stop at the elbow are for the gym only.

Dermablend—Olive Brown on the

Neck, upper chest, smeared and blended and patted

All over the face.

Grease ears.

Grease hands, especially

The right one.

Cover up hair falling out.

Fluff with pick and part

Wet curls to the left.

You can no longer pull off parting it down the middle.

Draw attention to your psoriasis first.

Make jokes in front of family or husband about not going out without your make-up.

Refer to yourself as the grizzly beast who doesn't want to scare the villagers without it.

Remember to use the right face lotion so your eyelids don't flake as much.

Tilt head up to most desirable side when taking pictures or before pressing "Join with Video" to head into the Zoom meeting.

Do pretend like you can buckle your seat on a plane— even when you can't.

You must lie to the flight attendant, cover your lap with a jacket or your purse

And lie

To yourself.

Wear headbands when you want to wear your hair straight back to cover the thinning patches.

Try not to feel your face burn and Do

Hold back tears when someone inevitably asks "What happened to your face, arms, hands, neck...?

Remember to have sweaters on hand.

Try to forget that makeup cannot hide it all.

Remember to be grateful for long sleeves and turtlenecks in the winter.

Do avoid hot water on your sores and quiet your cries when the heat hits it.

Do not mourn the years your skin was all the same color—

brown, dry, pink, splotchy, flaky and yellow and red
is your new color.

Do ignore blood stains on old T-shirts, bras and sheets.

Remember to brush off dead skin from desks, keyboards,
bedding and couch cushions.

Ignore the burnt and flaky skin while posing for pictures in the sun.

Do pretend your sores and scars don't bother you during sex.

Do wear girdles, control-top or big panties that cover your stomach
Do not scratch your earlobes too much in public because you will
bleed and expose your blood-soaked nailbeds.

Do not think about sores on the belly and the groin.

Do not erupt into tears when you find old photos of yourself before
the fall of 2014. It is unproductive.

Do not erupt into tears while reading these rules you have made.

Your survival rules.

Do not share your rules with the world.

Liberation

I want to be paid the highest compliment.

She. Is. Free.

I would be, too.

Free to take all my clothes off

On my balcony

In the dark

Brown full flesh kissing night air

Free to fall in

And out of love

As many times as

My big juicy heart pleases.

Free to swallow kiwis and mangoes

And cherries

Whole

Remnants dripping

Down my chin

Pulp lingering on lips

Free to

Laugh with eyes closed

And mouth wide open.

Free

To get it wrong

And let it go.

Someone said

Black women don't fall down.

Someone said

We've got to make the time then.

To fall down

Grow silent

Scream until

Throats ache

Cry without hiding tears

That splash and slide onto the chest.

Messy with no smooth edges

Nothing gets laid down.

I say

Only then

Would that freedom

Be

True.

Only then

Would that freedom

Be real.

Only then

Would that freedom

Be me.

My Need

The night I needed to learn

Began with Solange and her Black cowboys riding regally down Houston streets.

Her *When I Get Home* songs breaking the monotony of pasta cooking.

Audre Lorde's *Need* was read.

Brooklyn Public Library

Jameka, Keya, Liseli

You brought Audre's *Need* to me.

Toyin Salau's life was honored.

19 years and she was taken from us.

Where is my benevolent God?

Audre may have asked the same question

In 1979

About 12 Black women

In four months

In Boston

I needed to learn

And hear again

What I already knew.

Black women = Invisible

Pain ignored.

Birth movements, organize coalitions, speaking up = Threat

We become a threat to

Colonized mentality

Governments

Status quo

I wanted to say

"Black women are invisible and are perceived to be a threat
simultaneously. It is infuriating."

But it was their turn to speak.

You need to listen

To

Scholarly sisters

Gifting knowledge about mental health

Calling on ancestors

And the one lone brother's

Need

To protect his sisters
Closing with poetry

I was all rejoicing and
Vigorous head nodding

I no longer wanted to be connecting
from a screen.
I wanted to be in the room,
Be with these sisters.
My need was to
Shut the door behind me
With stacks of pages
And recordings
Of Black women.
I had homework to do.
My need became to
Write and read and shift
Perspective.
I wanted to ascend.
That night I was awash with the glow of Black cowboys,
transcendent music,
And Ms. Lorde setting
Everything
Ablaze
Inside of me.

Almost

I almost didn't write this week but then I thought of Toni Morrison, scribbling away on her yellow legal paper all those early mornings.

I almost didn't write this week but then I thought about how the sun burned my right breast through my T-shirt while I sunbathed on the balcony reading "Assata" on her birthday.

I almost didn't write this week but then I saw a towering tree in the distance that persistently leans left, bucking tradition of all the others that surround it.

I almost didn't write this week but then I saw my sister swing her twists while she gracefully spun and inverted on her pole, beckoning and inviting others to love themselves and her at.

I almost didn't write this week but then I thought of my husband's curls, shocks of black and silver, falling to the floor after holding it between my fingers, cutting new growth away.

I almost didn't write this week but then I remembered how I sobbed in the shower when I heard a stranger talk about her miscarriages and infertility.

I almost didn't write this week but then I opened a lipstick that made me smile wide when I painted my full lips the color of a deep red wine.

before

A wedge of orange, Chao cheese sandwiches dripping in oil, typing hesitant text messages, phone calls to a cousin, ribbons of creamy pasta wound around the hot tines of a silver fork, sex, rushed, fevered kisses, affirmations, song, a muted television, a screaming television, left and right thumbs on scroll, witty quotes, righteous anger, someone else's imaginary life, anticipation of grains of spicy rice and beans, onions greeting my lips, blame, approval, a like, a follow, sleep, acting out, rage and rage and rage, ranting to whomever is in the room or on the other end of the line, turbulent ocean waves raking against my thighs, ink pens, pencils, worn down, scribbling into the corners of pages—everything I turn to before seeking the face of God.

after

I want to tell you I am suddenly blooming in the wild of my insecurities, my mind no longer an agent of chaos.

I have surrendered to his will, lying prostrate on the floor.

But it is:

Silence, a hoarse voice, kneeling on the graying worn rug in our dusty guest bedroom with the pink walls, scraping the skin on my kneecaps, streaming tears in the bathroom at 2:38am because it finally dawned on me that I am your daughter and there is nothing I could do or say or think or ask or eat or drink or write or dream to separate me from

You.

All of the Flowers

The world needs all its flowers.

I heard it at the end of a meditation today.

I heard it, hurriedly grabbed a leopard print pen

That sits on our side table and scribbled it in a small orange memo book.

I then thought about all the things and the people that I consider "all the flowers."

Books. Heavenly books I have run into the arms of virtually every day these past few weeks.

The poinsettia kept all year long gifted from my mother-in-law that soaks in the sun. I absentmindedly reach out and stroke its leaves from time to time.

Our balcony at dusk where we have spent precious moments relishing silence, the comfort of our mismatched chairs and the sight of the tree where I often catch the same white cat perched on its branches.

My mother's text messages full of videos, jokes to make us laugh, inspire hope and advice to be as healthy and safe as possible.

Work. Knowing we are still able to help people, even over the phone and via email reminds me it isn't all over.

Friends. Knowing they are there is enough. Knowing they are there and safe is even better. I haven't done all the virtual "everythings," but I am still happy with the occasional phone calls and texts.

My family. I want them now more than ever.

They are my first flowers.

Other creators—artists of all stripes still finding their art in the midst of it. Even if their art is a reflection of their weariness in these times, I have fallen in love with their vulnerability.

The small business owners I watch hustling their wares online. I may not have hustle surging through my veins right now, but I respect their willingness and bravery to try do this in unprecedented times.

All the flowers taking care of the sick, carrying mail, delivering food, cleaning, stocking shelves, manning service stations, driving trucks and buses.

The flowers that bring us closer together and fight for those who voice has been muted or forgotten.

My husband's touch and voice remind me we walk together, never alone.

My Creator who made all of the flowers a reality.

The Island Answer

I do my job.

If I ask you to trust me for the next 20-30 minutes

Can I allow you to be seen?

I won't care about the length of your fingernails,
tattered T-shirt or your need for a haircut.

Can I tell you that you're in good hands?

Can I offer you just a little peace?

I'll do my best not to talk over you.

Let me give you my eye contact.

Ask how you feel this morning and

Listen to the answer.

Will you allow me to tell you that it will be hard,
but it won't be impossible?

I am only qualified to say this because I've seen it before.

This is not about what you've done, the fear of telling me

what you've done

Or even about me at all.

Yes, you did the hurting.

Yes, you were hurt.

I can't make you say it.

It's my job to ask.

I want you to know you are beyond numbers that identify you.

You are the sum parts of a whole.

You can be Whole.

If you did not believe it, you wouldn't be here.

Calling or coming inside was a first step.

You did that.

There is a "yes" you chose when "no" was an option.

I won't pretend to understand.

It's not my job.

It's not right to pretend I've walked in your shoes.

They are *your* shoes.

Please understand my perfectionism, my history of never wanting to be a disappointment and privilege landed me on this end of the line, on this side of the desk.

I can never allow myself to forget that.

When I am asked why I do what I do, how can I work with "such people," I ask them where do you believe they are supposed to go?

When they make a mistake, a series of mistakes, living with a well of regret, disease and trauma and spend months and years locked away, when they are free, where do you believe they are supposed to go?

Please tell me the name of the special island everyone should be banished to until the end of days after they've paid for their mistakes.

I'm waiting.

I'm waiting.

I'm waiting.

I'll save you some time.

The Island doesn't exist.

Good Girl

I learned about the mechanics—the body.

But I did not learn the heart—the emotion.

I kept my knees closed so they could not be pried open.

I knew there was power in my "No."

When I was 14, I was teased from white and Black people

For dating a blond, white boy.

So, I let him go.

A couple of years later, he saw me in a department store.

I was fuller.

He told my friend I was still pretty, even with all the extra me.

My first real kiss came from him in a department store,
hidden in the luggage section.

"Did I do it right?" I asked.

A tall handsome chocolate boy who scooped ice cream with a name I liked more than him—his first and last.

He kissed me on his father's couch.

He kissed me in the moonlight behind the brick beam in a shopping center.

He kissed me in the passenger seat of my red station wagon with the silver luggage racks.

I flushed as he lightly kissed the part of my breast that peeked through the top of my blouse. I sang SWV's "Weak" on the way home because I thought I was finding out what love is.

He loved someone else.

A man who told me if I lived in his neighborhood I would have been taken a long time ago.

The boys in my neighborhood must have been sleeping.

He had a pit bull tattooed on his chest, worked security and often told me he loved my voice,

thought I was a diamond.

We fell apart.

No one would really look at me for a while after that.

I was at school, in between classes where everyone played pool.

A man approached me, asked me for my number.

Was he talking to me?

I didn't see myself then.

I was still waiting to be seen.

A young man with a nice face and broken English
who lived with three other people.

We were smitten with each other.

Or so I thought

One night when no one was home,

He cooked peppers so hot

He asked me not to touch them

And then he laid me down

And kissed me.

Touched me with residue on his fingertips

Instinct

Moved me to clasp my hands over my vagina.

His hands roved; pepper juice-stained fingers roamed

He told me not to fear.

He wouldn't go anywhere

He was not allowed.

I don't remember much about that night.

I woke up the next day, peed and in pain, burning.

When I told him that night or the next,

He laughed at me,

Asked me if I remembered

Going where he wasn't allowed.

Was this a joke?

He kept laughing and said No.

I shook my head back and forth.

No was on repeat.

My reality kept crashing down on me, a metal grinding against
my teeth,

smashing down on my brain

and it was hot and no.

No one was going to snap me out of this, jolt me out of this reality.

The one where this man, this boy with a white-toothed pretty smile
told me that he....

And when he saw that I wasn't smiling, too,

He recanted.

The fast-paced furious breathing slowed, and I immediately believed.

Or told him I did. I couldn't bear not to believe.

The girl in the pew couldn't bear not to believe he was playing a
cruel joke.

The girl who promised her Mom and God and told her friends
and family she always said No.

And then others came.

A gorgeous dreadlocked man sat in a corner,

strummed a guitar for me.

Then laid me down, tracing my areolas and my navel with fingers
across my clothed body

And everything I thought I knew became fuzzy and dared
to float away.

But I could still call myself a good girl.

But whenever a "he" said *You're pretty* or

I like the way your hair swings (freshly after being relaxed)

I could tell them my knees couldn't be pried open

But take everything else.

Didn't you call me pretty?

Didn't you tell me there was something special about me?

You don't have to say, "I love you."

And after every stand-up, disappearance

I learned to blame it on those locked knees.

Puffed up and mighty with my power to deny.

Someone

I would replay.

Flirtations, long walks, play fights that ended in mussed hair, shrieks and giggles, drinks shared, drunken, nonsensical fights at parties, him grabbing me from someone I was dancing with, telling me he didn't want me but then seeking me all over again, working together, him creeping up behind me as I shelved books, so we could stand in place, not be seen by others, but silently pressed against one another, napping on his couch, breathing softly as he nestled into my chest, drunk stumbling to my door, the one long slow dance to Brian McKnight songs as he sang softly into my ear, the one time he cooked me breakfast, told me he didn't care that I had a boyfriend, could he be my someone on the side, told me I was one of two people who really knew him, the first time we kissed, the last time we kissed in his mother's basement. His girlfriend's picture was upstairs in a frame, face down on his dresser. I didn't care. I was there first.

I would replay

Him.

Years later

I would dream of running into him again, look for his truck in cities

Where he did not live.

I could never call him mine.

Didn't tell him I was a good girl for years.

I wanted to be a mystery to him.

I wanted to be an obsession.

I may have been at one time,

But he forgot me.

Long before I forgot him.

Our last conversation

"I loved you back then."

I said I loved back you then but what I meant to say was

I loved you. I still love you.

I wanted to tell him how he made me feel

When we were in his bed and he lifted my body in the air

Like he was bench pressing me

How I loved stroking his hair when he fell asleep on me

That I pretended not to be as interested because

I feared

My locked knees

Driving him to other women.

I feared

the drinking, addiction

rejection

But the truth is

It was never me.

He visited me in my dreams

Less than 3 years after he left this plane,

Two days before I walked down the aisle.

He pulled me into my bathroom, one I hadn't seen in years.

And told me it was ok.

Whatever I thought we were

It wasn't.

I had barely thought about him in two years

And here he was.

Pulling me close

And pushing me

Towards

The only man I

Could be sure

Loved me as much

As I loved him.

Time in the Kitchen

I am waiting for my husband to come home with bunches of greens from his mother's house.

We are going to rinse the earth from the leaves, smash and peel garlic cloves, dice red onions, sprinkle spices and boil and simmer.

Our fingers will be coated with spice and juice.

We will stand in the kitchen, keeping an eye over the heat, nostrils tickled by the aroma.

The chit chat will be idle.

I will tell him how delicious it will be — our feast.

Occasionally, I will inch closer to him, crane my neck, pout my lips and his head will bend down to receive

Me.

We do this.

One time

We made love

To classical music

And we laughed

After we caught

Our breath.

We asked

Who does this?

We do.

We do this.

We found a scene

From a movie.

I was the coy but sexy temptress waiting at the bar.

He was a local boy looking for local trouble.

And we clumsily became actors.

We laughed.

Who does this?

We do.

We do this.

When my skin fell apart and I often left traces of my pretty brown on the bathroom floor, in the sheets and on the furniture, he undressed me, applied salve all over my body—back, arms, neck, breasts, legs, ears and told me he wishes he could take it all away from me.

And I asked

Who does this?

He does.

He does this.

He does Love.

Buffalo and Helicopters

They were in the distance, black dots becoming closer and taking shape.

Buffalo.

I drew a sharp breath.

I had never been that close. My husband was driving and pointing. I was always scared of him doing that, taking his eyes off the road, disregarding my pleas for laser-like focus on the road.

We had just come from Red Rocks Amphitheater.

My husband said we were to be Black black Camaro people in Colorado.

We had driven, at a crawling pace per my request, per my quickened heartbeat's request, up a mountain with its narrow road, to witness the majesty of these red rocks. The engine was all rumble and growl which turned me into a 4-year-old girl again, hiding behind my uncle's legs during the premiere of "Thriller."

I was peeking through legs then.

I was peeking through fingers now, pleading with God to make me a brave woman who defiantly sticks her head out of the window, letting the snowflakes dance across her tongue and begs her husband to rev the engine, go a little faster.

At the top, we sat where thousands had before us, decades before us. On those red rocks steps, the snow quietly fell, and my imagination twisted an empty stage into Bob Marley shaking his locs, singing a redemption song and Santana wailing on his guitar, echoing into the perfect sky.

So now you see

Buffalo in the distance should have meant nothing but there was a desire to leap from the car and run through the fields to touch their skin

if they would let me.

To look into their eyes.

Would they scare me, or would I be scary to them?

Would they understand the image of a chubby Black woman with a curly afro, crimson-stained lips and thick brown fingers reaching out towards them?

The moment passed quickly.

We drove into Boulder and did not speak of them for the rest of our stay. During the last few minutes of the flight back home, I gazed out of the window, watching our descent into Richmond.

I spied a field of black dots and the shapes crystallized as we flew closer.

Helicopters.

I needed my eyes to swim in a field of buffalo.

I wanted to take leave of my breath one more time.

The Butterfly and the Lion

I am thinking of burning it all down.

The version of me who is running from everything I ever wanted.

I am thinking of torching it and watching its splendid ashes float to the ground.

Every time I step outside of my chalk-lined box or circle forever made around me. That is what I am doing.

I am lighting the match. I am knocking down trees with my bare fists, not caring how bloodied my knuckles become.

Because I get to be the bulldozer and not the bulldozed.

You may think it takes an act of gigantic proportion but to me, it is whipping around Manhattan on tired feet last week

or opening my mouth and letting the words fall out, letting them hang and sit for my sister to hear, the words I have longed to tell her for almost 2 years—I miss you.

The act of taking this class and not apologizing for sitting here on a Wednesday morning.

Every new thing, everything I hadn't seen myself doing burns it down, slays a monster, feels like I could give a butterfly the strength of a lion.

It closes the curtain of who I thought I was, what I "should" be doing, fear of what someone would say,

or how lost I would become.

That curtain doesn't get to come back up.

Epiphany

An invitation to their inner sanctum, a darkened dance studio with poles and lush fabric cascading down from the ceiling.

Seated on a leather couch, *An Untamed State* lying in my lap.

For two hours, I watched as a group of women twisted and flexed their bodies to pop and trap,

swung their figures to melody and bass.

I observed women opening and closing their palms—Clap clap.

Lifting each other up, there was no collapse.

I spied the sinewy, willowy, muscled curvy Beautiful slick with sweat move in and out of time.

My eyes burned and there were tears edging its way out of the corners and gliding down my cheeks.

I think this had been coming on for a while, the tide coming in.

I felt it coming when I walked out of my sister's house and kept moving for an hour, drowning the world out, even the wind whistling through the trees. And then when I held my nephew's basketball in my hands, palms covering the leather and I raised my arms, shooting again and again until they ached.

I missed doing something

just for me.

A Cleansing

My love has not been devoured by Wolf

But he has tried, licked his chops, snarled and prowled, circling him

Many mornings, many nights.

He took my love from our bed.

I wandered to find him

Under attack.

I had to dial the three numbers

I resisted over the years.

I was always able to get to him in time,

Gather him into my car

Just a short drive away

He could always hold on

But on that day

It was too late for gathering.

Wolf has forced me to sleep on backbreaking cots

Quiver underneath thin sheets

Amid beeping machines

Ask myself is the brave face

Coming across as panicked actress, tripping predictably in the woods because

Wolf has finally come for me.

Entrenched me in daydreams

Where I hike Crabtree Falls again

Pause long enough to snap photos of flowing waters.

I am transfixed.

I become a lonely painter on a retreat,

Biking and hitch hiking to Menemsha Beach on Martha's Vineyard

Admiring the sunset

Tangerine and coral swallowed by the blanket of night

I have been told

I am craving a cleansing.

Wash me.

Make me a new thing.

So, I will be safe

Away

from Wolf

Etch A Sketch

I maneuvered the white knobs in my head over the years.
Dexterous hands that exist only in my imagination
Sketched brows, thick, heavy, hairy

Noses with width and forgettable nostrils
Lashes so long they rested on the apples of the cheeks.
Narrow hands, bony fingers, wide feet
An afro
Strands that are coarse, curly, silky, kinky spring to life on this
One head
A buck-toothed smile

He will need braces.

Diagnoses made, the other side of 37 reached and

I could not get my fingers to work,

Manipulate the knobs

Not even where my dreams reside

I picked up the gray, flat screen with the red plastic frame

And shook it

Until

He disappeared

And I crumbled.

The aluminum powder and the beads

Dissipated

Because he

Was never real.

Because he

Was never

Ours.

Awakening

Awakening

Takes on the shape

Of the skin

You are fitting it into

In this skin

I never wait

To throw axes

Climb rocks

Swing around poles

Dance barefoot on hard wood

Sweat and strain to stretch and hold poses

Heal in salt caves

With pink ambient lighting

Curl my fingers

Around bars

Slam ropes

Undress

slip into an orb

Close the door over my nude body

And float

Welcoming darkness and silence

Beckoning psychedelic vision

My awakening

Does not wait

For my torso this

My legs that

My arms this

My skin that

I've done my waiting.

It aches to wait.

It hurts to wait.

When you can no longer sleep.

She Lives Here

Joy lives here even when I suspect she has lost her way, broken the GPS, slipped her bra out from her sleeves and took a long nap at a rest stop.

Joy lives here even when I am calling repairmen, performing feats of verbal gymnastics trying to fix this house so I can finally say good-bye to it.

Joy lives here even when I am dead tired and on my umpteenth week of forgetting to take all my vitamins.

Joy lives here even when I am terrified my words will never be embraced or I will never be understood.

Joy lives here even though the fullness of my Black womanhood is in question—my competency, the bounds of my love, intellect and the sanctity of my vulnerability.

Joy lives here because I ask her to move in every day. Move into the creases and the folds and skin and the breath.

Joy, I ask you to come home.

Joy, I ask you to stay.

Colophon

She Lives Here was typeset in Freight Text and Neue Kabel.

Freight Text is a serif typeface designed by Joshua Darden and published through GarageFonts in 2005. Freight is an extremely versatile superfamily with many different versions available, making it suitable for a wide range of typographic challenges. It is the type family used by the National Museum of African American History and Culture in Washington D.C.

Kabel is a geometric sans-serif typeface designed by Rudolf Koch in 1927. It has been published by various foundries over the years under different names, including Geometric 231, Koblenz Serial and TS Koblenz. ITC published ITC Kabel in 1975 with an exaggerated x-height, which was typical of the phototype of that era. In 2016, a comprehensive update of Kabel was designed by Marc Schütz and published through Linotype as Neue Kabel (used on the cover and section titles), in nine weights with matching italics.

She Lives Here was designed by Llewellyn Hensley & Content–Aware Graphic Design—**content-aware.design.**

Thank you
for supporting *Unzipped*

Our project is made possible by readers like you. We are infinitely grateful to our patrons who make it possible for us to continue publishing urgent, brave, and true stories! To learn more about supporting us through our subscription program, our online litmag, classes, and workshops, visit **lifein10minutes.com/unzipped.** We would love to write, read, and (metaphorically) unzip with you.

Issue 3 will take you into the landscape of four women's stories: Paula Gillison, Mary Jo McLaughlin, Lisa Loving, and Sema Wray. Within these brave, true, and unzipped stories, you will find women with sass and bootys and unholy motives who journey through bad boys and even worse men; pastel chicks and mother assassins, tenderly care for wounded abusers; wander nomadic teenage treks through broken glass and hell-bent hormones; and the darkest parts of love—be it from family, friendship, or religion.